Watering Can

CAROLINE BIRD, who was born in 1986, was a winner of the Foyles Young Poets of the Year Award in 1999 and 2000, and the Peterloo Poets Competition for Young Poets in 2002, 2003 and 2004. She was shortlisted for the Geoffrey Dearmer Prize in 2001 and won a major Eric Gregory Award in 2002. Her first collection, *Looking Through Letterboxes*, was published by Carcanet Press in 2002. She was shortlisted for the Dylan Thomas Prize for Young Writers for her second collection, *Trouble Came to the Turnip* (Carcanet 2006). Caroline Bird is also a playwright: she has had two rehearsed readings at the Royal Court, three student productions in Oxford and one at the Edinburgh Fringe in 2009. She has read and discussed her poetry on many BBC radio programmes, including *Finelines*, *Woman's Hour* and *The Verb*, and the BBC commissioned her short story 'Sucking Eggs', broadcast in 2003. She wrote and performed two films for the recent BBC poetry season, and has read her poetry at a range of venues and festivals, including the Royal Festival Hall, Hay, Cheltenham, Ledbury, Manchester and Glasgow. Caroline Bird is an enthusiastic leader of poetry workshops in schools and a regular teacher at the Arvon Foundation. She is currently the president of the Oxford Poetry Society.

T0164297

CAROLINE BIRD

Watering Can

CARCANET

First published in Great Britain in 2009 by
Carcanet Press Limited
Alliance House
Cross Street
Manchester M2 7AQ

A CIP catalogue record for this book is available from the British Library
ISBN 978 1 84777 088 2

The publisher acknowledges financial assistance from Arts Council England

Typeset by XL Publishing Services, Tiverton
Printed and bound in England by SRP Ltd, Exeter

for my Dad

Acknowledgements

With thanks to the editors of the following publications in which some of these poems first appeared: *Poetry London, Bat City Review, City State: New London Poetry, Oxford Poetry* 2008 and 2009.

The poem 'Women in Progress' was commissioned by BBC Radio 4's *Woman's Hour*.

Contents

The Videos

Someone gave me a video of your entire life.
There's a twist at the end
when you discover that you and your mother
are actually the same person
and I drop out of the picture in about two months' time,
only to return as a busboy
who steals your handbag and uses your passport
to smuggle loads of rabid dogs into the city.
I'm one of those strange comic characters with a dead tooth.
You get married to an organisation junkie
who sells your hair to buy a stash of pocket calculators
and your daughter falls in love with me
and I break her heart over a plate of tagliatelle,
then you get addicted to cough mixture
and sleep in a sodden nightie with the windows open
before buying a lovely house in the country.

Last Tuesday

I miss my Tuesday so much. I had a Tuesday
today, but it wasn't the same. It tasted funny.
There were signs it had already been opened.
The seal was broken. Someone had poisoned it
with Wednesday-juice. In fact, I think today
was actually Wednesday, but the government
was trying to pass it off as Tuesday by putting
my tennis lesson back a day, rearranging the
tea towels. I sent a letter to MI5 and the CIA
and the rest. I know they have my Tuesday.
They're keeping it for experiments because it
was so freakishly happy. I was smiling in my
sleep when two men in body-sized black socks
stole it from my bedside table. It was here.
It was right here. But when I woke up, it was
gone. Their Wednesday stole my Tuesday.
Their frigging totalitarian cloud-humped shit-
swallower of a Wednesday stole my innocent
Tuesday. And now it's just getting ridiculous:
the days change every week, it's like an avalanche.
As soon as I start to get the hang of a day, learn
the corridors, find my locker key, the bell goes
and suddenly it's Thursday, or Friday, but not
last Friday or Thursday, oh no, these are different
ones with kneecaps like pustules, gangly eyes:
you never know which way they'll lunge.

In the Lost Property Office, I held up the queue.
'It's greenish,' I told the attendant, 'with a mouth
that opens to a courtyard.' But they only had a box
of wild Fridays some lads had misplaced in Thailand.
(I took a couple of those, for the pain.) Then I
gave up. I ignored the days, and they ignored me.
I drank Red Bull in the ruins of monasteries,
flicking through calendars of digitally enhanced dead
people: Gene Kelly downloading a remix
of 'Singin' in the Rain' on his slimline Apple Mac.

No one gives a damn about time anymore. Happy hour
lasts all afternoon. You can put a hat on a corpse
and send it to work. You can bury a baby.
Hip counsellors in retro tweed jackets keep
telling me to look ahead. There'll be other Tuesdays
to enjoy, they say, new Tuesday pastures. It's a lie.
I found my Tuesday in someone else's bed.
Its chops were caked in velvet gel and its voice
had corrupted. It pretended to be a Saturday,
but I could see myself reflected in its eyes, a younger
me, tooting the breeze with a plastic trombone.
'I'm sorry,' said my Tuesday, pulling its hand out
of a woman, 'I didn't mean to let you down, but
I couldn't stay perfect forever, you were suffocating me.
Even sacred memories need to get their rocks off.'

Peaked

Popped out,
showered off,
took my burden
down to the play school,
bought a Lego mansion
they never finished building,
paid through the neck for twenty grams
of glitter glue, hit the chocolate milk,
learnt Danish with the purpose of reading
The Ugly Duckling in the original,
didn't see it through, washed-up, my fifth birthday bombed,
'I preferred your early work,' said a girl with measles,
'it was rawer, richer, these cupcakes seem hackneyed',
superiors tried to placate me with kazoos,
plasticine crumbled to luminous ash,
my novelette about the hippo
was mistook for a comedy,
Miranda, that cunning bitch,
read her poem in class,
'My doll', it was called,
pretentious crap:
immature,
clunky.

Wild Flowers

I will be sober on my wedding day,
my eggs uncracked inside my creel,
my tongue sleeping in her tray.

I will lift my breast to pay
babies with their liquid meal,
I will be sober on my wedding day.

With my hands, I'll part the hay,
nest inside the golden reel,
my tongue sleeping in her tray.

I'll dance with cows and cloying grey,
spin my grassy roulette wheel,
I will be sober on my wedding day.

I'll crash to muddy knees and pray,
twist the sheets in tortured zeal,
my tongue sleeping in her tray.

Church bells shudder on the bay,
fingered winds impel the deal:
I will be sober on my wedding day,
my tongue sleeping in her tray.

The Golden Kids

She became an usher to an usher in an ushering firm
for failed burglars with tiny torches
waving fools up the runway in theatrical darkness.

He had a baby by accident,
a blank colour house like a primary school foyer, hiding
from his baby, knees up in the Wendy house,
reading and rereading the alcohol proverb.

He joined a charity organisation.
Oh, the willow tree shelter of other people's problems,
whining up around you like sticks of faded light.

She found happiness in love, of all places,
happiness in love. Oh mourn the happy.

He waited for his mum to die
then started playing drums in a band
called 'mad for the mad', wearing eyeshadow.

She fell for a millionaire
and locked herself in a house with cocaine
and playing cards and rang me occasionally
for stories of the city.

She became an astronomer without a telescope,
writing 'Today will be a lucky day, but unlucky
things might happen', bought a bong and settled down.

She walked in on a friend having sexual intercourse
with a dog and nothing was said except
'That's not your dog.'

She left the mental asylum to work in mental health care.
He left the rack to join the army.
She left the heroin to write a book.

She drank a small espresso in a café in Paris
forever, surrounded by gorillas with hamburger breath
and notes on failure to perform in bed.

He sat on the floor and waited for the surrealists
to convert his empty flat into an Indian elephant.

She bought a surfboard decorated with a painting
of the sunrise, propped it up like an ironing board
against the French windows and demanded it
make her carefree.

He became the thought of his wife in a bar with a man.

He became the thought of a man on a beach
at six in the morning with a broken metal detector.

He became the thought of a man on pills without pills
just going insane.

She became her own bearded Marilyn.

She went to build an orphanage on the other side of the planet
and left her goldfish behind. By goldfish, I mean children.

She had a school reunion: they wore their school jumpers,
they drank the old beer and blackcurrant and talked
about clinical depression as if it were a hip new motorcycle
they'd all invented together. *I've just bought the latest pillbox,*
such delicate workmanship, easy-open catch, a sturdy velvet base.
Steel grey is such a fashionable colour, don't you think?

He became a soft acoustic singer–songwriter and wrote
we've only got one life, my baby, so pass me the knife, my baby,
and I'll carve you a picture of my soft acoustic strife,
then floated off the stage to stick his soft acoustic penis in a groupie.

She became a state of the art homosexual
and silhouetted herself in tender smoke
with a book of women poets and a black and white film collection
of female erotica, and a defining haircut and a London apartment
with tapestries on the wall – woven by Third World women –
and put a woman in her satin double bed and used the word vulva
in normal conversations and caught a plane to San Francisco
to parade the streets with a whistle around her neck,
wondering why the blue sky was so earnest
when all of nature's creatures united in tedium and she was still
so uncomfortable in cotton.

He became a state of the art heterosexual and cooked himself
strong dinners of fish and new potatoes, thinking
his arms would be so muscular if he was Australian.

She became the memory of six teenagers on a sweet tobacco sofa
in a crumbling house, saving their beer-caps, glad to be
contemplating suicide because the future is healing
the acne on their skin and they are the golden kids.

Impartial Information

Police cars are available, medical attention
is available. Hostels, hairdressers, health spas
are available. Fire engines are available.
Group therapy, colour therapy, cognitive,
aversion and alternative therapy, acupuncture
and cupping are available. Anger management,
drink, drug, rack and ruin, gambling and marriage
counselling are available. Yellow Pages
are available, runaway helplines, gay and lesbian
switchboards, national debt-line, Sexual
Health Direct, coastguards are available. Talk-shows,
blood donors, legal advice, Methadone, some kind
of guidance, mostly, a compassionate friend,
a bit of loose change are available. Air and space
and pub toilets are available. Greenery,
mountains, Neighbourhood Watch, local councils,
peace are available. Bereavement care,
Disabled Living Foundation helplines, love
are available. Happiness is available. So
when you entertain the thought
of falling to your knees in a final plea,
it's not for the lack of
availability.

Expecting Rain

in memory of John

Jenny dolled herself up for the funeral
in fishnet socks and winkle-picker shoes
and the pink umbrella he'd bought her.

His ex-wife
howled by the graveside
as the earth pinched over,
but Jenny held her pink umbrella.

After, there was a knees-up
in the rugby club,
and the 'silly mares' from work,
wine-dark behind keening veils,
tackled the throat
of her turquoise shawl,
abusing coupled words:
'send off',
'good times'.

Me and my new partner
springy in our trainers,
went round for dinner on Monday.
Jenny said, 'Do I look sixty-six?'
and we laughed.
'With pins like yours? No chance.'

Today, Jenny tippled beer
with her pink umbrella
and gossiped by his grave
about that stupid Humanist speaker
whose phone rang twice
and his bloody ex-wife with her purple face.

Elsewhere, in a trendy park,
we aired our teeth under a drizzled sky,
elderly cars parked
exhausted pipe to bumper.
I wrung your hand,
laundered our many, fragrant vows.

We sprinted home, windswept,
draped our gloves
on the radiator, undressed.
I stood, embraced,
in your tent of flesh, my pink umbrella.

The Monogamy Optician

He held up laminated pictures of can-can dancers.
He drew a dot on the wall and said, 'Is it a foetus?'
He said, 'Hold your head back like you would at the hairdresser.'
He studied my retinas through a hole in a hammer.

He said, 'Unfaithfulness is a product of surplus sight,
it's the bridesmaid in the corner of the wedding photo.'
He said, 'Since my peripheries were surgically removed,
I've only had eyes for my wife. It's the miracle cure.'

He sent for his nurse in the living-mushroom apron.
She said, 'Your peripheries will be surgically removed.'
I said, 'Do you never sneak a glimpse on the underground?'
She caught my words in the gas-mask like a baseball glove.

My grandparents had similar treatment in the fifties,
though the peripheries were sliced by hand, before lasers.
Happy couples swooning the beach in their padded glasses,
colliding with bollards and donkeys and news-stands and deckchairs.

That night I flounced in: 'Honey, I went to the optician
and they fixed my wandering eyes, look I'll prove it.'
I dragged us to a sexy bar called the Kaleidoscope,
trained my gaze on your face like a sparrow in a neck-brace.

When we split, I returned to the opticians in a sulk.
No cash refunds. The machines looked rusty in the daylight.
He said, 'It's not our fault if your peripheries grow back.'
I trudged home through the park with all the daffodils and stuff.

The Oven Glove Tree

A woman I could talk to in a warmer season
is selling oven gloves printed with the logo
of a banjo-fusion-techno band.
She has strapped the oven gloves
to the prongs of a hatstand
and erected it outside the pissed-off train station.
Big spongy hands waving.
The commuters are literally ducking.
They don't want to fall in love with the oven glove tree,
not today, not on the 5000th day of their temporary job.

Wait.
A neon man just descended his bicycle.
Maybe an oven glove would be nice for Christmas?
A Kensington wife spent her poodle's
clothing allowance. Maybe it would be nice.
A tramp coughed up. Oven glove woman
is bouncing the change in her bumbag.
I bet she's some kind of spiritual healer or herbal florist
in her spare time. I bet she could lay hands
on a cripple and make him dance.
I bet she could do it with oven gloves on.

Maybe she could skip me back to my schooldays
when pain was still something illegal
we did at weekends over a few sly beers.
Maybe she and I could open an oven glove company,
so socialist types would never burn their hands
on their space-cakes.

Sold out.
The plastic hatstand is folded by a hinge
in its middle, stuffed in a gig bag. The woman counts
the cash, puts the notes in an envelope and stomps
through the barriers to the District line.
I make a benchmark in the frost and sit down.

Bow Your Head and Cry

When the ambulance finally rocked up,
its bouncy wheels rolling merrily over the cobbles,
our love was barely breathing.
I had been blowing into its mouth,
but I must have blown too hard.
Our love had swallowed its tongue. The poor dear.
All the little old ladies, looking out from their teashops,
were muttering 'What a shame,'
and 'It was so young.'
'Shut up,' I said, and slapped one of them.
'It's not dead yet. Look. Its legs are still moving.'
Just then, its legs stopped moving.
The paramedics put on their duffel coats
because it had started to drizzle.
'Shall we get out the stretcher,' they asked,
'or would that be a bit pointless?'
I lay down beside our love
and held its teeny hand.
You weren't even there to witness the passing.

Head Girl

for Miss Elizabeth Candy

I had a headmistress who was more liberal than her laws,
she had to tease the toupees of members of the board,
shine the boots of 4 x 4s, wreath their passengers,
dole out the assembly prayer like it was one of hers.

The deputy, on the other hand, haemorrhaged if you swore,
checked your skirt with a ruler, supported the war,
but my headmistress met Sophia Loren in 1954.
Past six, her cigarillo smoke jazzed up the corridor.

She planned to emigrate with her partner, defrock
the priestess mums who trailed her round the shops
to bless her trolley-contents, elevate their sprogs
(as if getting them their sodding grades wasn't enough).

She planned a clock-defying journey to a piano bar where
women of a certain type, the Old School Debonair,
who never married, luckily, and found their joys elsewhere,
would tryst in tilted bowler hats, reciting Baudelaire.

But the league tables are merciless, they hound you till you die
then conservatise your spirit at that bake-sale in the sky.
The deputy always said I was unable to comply
with the Head's commands. Au contraire! I obeyed her wry smile.

Road Signs

on the way to my work

You were travelling a grey motorway.
You had a baby in your lap
with enormous green eyes
and a scarily large head.
You parked the car in a lay-by, sat on the roof,
held her high like a trophy,
joked, 'One day all of this will be yours.'

Then you crunched the leaves from the trees
into a mess of green and said, 'These are leaves.'
Baby said, 'Show me something else.'
You showed your baby the ocean
and baby said, 'Salty.'
You showed your baby mud
and baby covered herself in mud.
You showed your baby a grown man
and baby said, 'Let's give some green
to that man and some ocean and some mud.'
So you did. Then you showed your baby tears
and baby said, 'Ocean?'
Then you showed your baby blood
and baby said, 'Salty,'
and you said, 'Don't drink that,'
and baby said, 'Muddy man,'
and baby said, 'Bloody leaves,'
and baby said, 'The ocean is a green man with salty blood,'
and you recognised your baby's madness.

Now I am a young woman
I travel the grey motorway alone
and women who are not my mother
teach me grey, acidic truths:
weather girls trapped in thick glass buildings,
situation comedies with boldly coloured sofas,
mini-markets flourishing in meteorite craters.

I pop the cork on my strange vinegar bottle,
try to become unrecognisable.

But when I return,
the swaddling-wraps still steaming on the floor
from when I evaporated, my mother
pours green tea, shows me the tyre-marks on her wrist –
souvenirs from the grey motorway.
Then she points at the sky and says,
'Those are clouds,'
then she takes me outside and says
'This is sunlight,'
then she pushes me down a well and says
'That is darkness,'
and I mean to say, 'Obviously,'
but I say, 'Bandages, griddle and ouch,'
I say, 'Griddle my bandages,'
I say, 'Sunlight my ouch,'
I say, 'Bandaged clouds griddle darkness with sun,'
and I run inside to find a pen
and my mother shouts, 'A is for Apple!'
and I write and I write and I write
our sweet green poem.

Bright Winter Mornings in Oxford Town

The milk's run out, the scholars are weeping.
'The cleaners came and stole the goddamn milk.'
The cleaners serve to rearrange their filth.
The coffee smells like dead scholars seeping.
'The cleaners can't replace a toilet roll.'
The soap dispenser's hollow once again.
A scholar moves his bowels just like his pen,
with grace and grunts and a personal goal.

Remember when I drank that rum and black
with dirty lips so dumb and kissable?
Now I'm another gown upon the rack.
My sheets are bleached by the invisible.
After I bathe, I neatly shave my crack.
I dress. I take my library books back.

Stage Kiss

The writer wrote a play about his girlfriend
and he looked at the actress looking at the actor
and he thought, 'I wish someone would look at me like that.'

The actor playing the boyfriend
looked at the actress looking at him
and he thought, 'I wish someone would look at me like this.'

The actress playing the girlfriend
wetted her lips for the stage kiss
and she thought, 'I wish someone would kiss me like her.'

The writer's girlfriend watched the actress
kissing the actor playing her boyfriend
and she thought, 'It must be thrilling to be an actress.'

The director kissed the actress backstage
and he thought, 'Her kiss in the scene
was more realistic than this one.'

The audience leant in for the kiss:
I wish my life looked like this play.

Seesaw

During your baby-scan, I'm on
the 'It's a Small World' ride at Disneyland
cruising tiddly topography in a pinkish boat.
Dummies with maracas doing the plastic-polka
that never leads to funny business.
At twenty-one, I'm elderly for this.

While the doctor jellies your lump,
my little brother – now eighteen,
with a good set of shoulders – buys
an ironic Buzz Lightyear gun, ironically
waves to Aladdin's float, holds hands
with mum – ironically – in the manufactured snow.

My best friend is having a baby boy
and I'm on the Tower of Terror ride
dropping thirteen floors with a seatbelt on.
After childhoods spent outgrowing – ferociously –
soft drinks and school, you're counting piggies
on miniature hands and I'm twirling in a tea-cup,
an honorary child.

In my training-bra, I fought hard to be real.
Just like Tilly from nursery who filled
her doll's nappy with peanut butter (crunchy),
I got published during puberty, crayoned
wrinkles on my face, while you matured naturally.

Remember when you unwrapped a tampon
in the pub and dunked it in your pint?
I went red, but you clapped
for the brave white worm, absorbing Snakebite.
We were like Thelma and Louise
without the car.

Now you're ballooning in that box
of a town, telling your on-off chap
to stop laughing at toilet jokes and be a man.
I'm regressing, meanwhile, on Thunder Mountain.
There must be a pulley-system:
one of us grows, the other shrinks.

Penelope's Chair

I wore inedible knickers, hung out with penitent monks
until one whipped out his branch. 'I'm a married woman!' I yelped,
'Let go of my marvellous breasts!' I unearthed my wedding dress,
started wearing it to clubs, raving with glow-sticks and scruples.

I went to the adult bookshop for a book on adulthood
but all they had was *Threesome in Reno*, and *Cream-gartered Sue*.
What's a novice monogamist to do? My love was at sea.
Scruples splattered the sand like broken shells. My spyglass got bust.

By the time the boat came home, laden with stuffed bears
                                                  and stuffed hearts,
I was fending them off with a screwdriver. Packs of suitors
pressing fliers into my hands outside Sainsbury's: 'Choose me!'
My sailor dripped on our porch-step, his scruples round his ankles.

'Where the fuck have you been?' There wasn't time for archery,
I took his boat: 'I'll be back in ten years, see how you like it.'
Like whores behind beaded curtains, mermaids snickered in the rain.
I survived by peeling monkey skulls with a bladed scruple.

A decade passed. I turned around. He was living with his mum.
We hunched over a plate of chocolate biscuits, like old junkies.
Our elbows went weak at the knees, a tear curled up in my ear.
Partied out, we grow scruples and watercress in the window.

D.N. eh?

You can live your life, I'm giving it back to you.
I tried to wear it like a jumpsuit
but the leather and the tweed kept chafing my thighs.
The drycleaners didn't recognise the material.
I tried to roll it like a barrel down the hills of my hometown
but its corners kept cutting the cobbles.
It flattened my family house with its strange swinging boulders.
Who the hell designed this machine?
It kept shrinking and stretching. One minute
I could slot it into my gob like a tooth, the next minute
it was driving my school bus into the lake.
I adjusted all the straps, the gears, peeled off the lewd labels
but your life was a bugger to steer.
I ended up dumping it in theatre cloakrooms
then losing the ticket. People kept delivering it
back to my door in bizarrely shaped packages.
Little boys on push-bikes chucked it over my fence
like a rolled-up newspaper. My neighbour
gave me a dog leash for my birthday. Every Joanna
and Joe Bloggs had a piece to say about me
and your life. I became the keeper of keys.
The local police took your name off the missing persons list
and onto my postbox. Your life was officially mine.
I tried to plant it in the garden, one big toe
poking up through the soil like a potato,
but the trees started squealing like pigs,
my water sprinkler slept through its timer, your life
fiddled with the phone lines, treated my clothes horse
like a bungee. Frankly, it cut and bruised itself
crawling behind those skirting-boards
like a blood-soaked ghost. It couldn't even stir soup.
Useless, it was useless.

I placed it on my eyeball like a contact lens
and started seeing things: saints with erections
playing netball with elephants. Your life was madder
than a mushroom. So I took it to a prostitute.

A capable, clever prostitute who used to work in a nursery.
I said, 'This life is too much for me.'
I gave her three hundred pounds.
I watched from the chaise longue.
She pouted her pouch and thrusted her thing
but your life just shrank, right there, inside its trousers,
welded itself to the wall like a poster, prayed
like a Christian, shook like a skull and cried out my name.
The prostitute had to put her breasts away
and read the first chapter of *Huckleberry Finn*,
doing all the voices, until it breathed again.

That evening, I found a stash of colouring books
under its hammock. Your life had been finger-painting
secretly in the bathroom. Those rubber duckies
didn't just appear, it bought them from the toyshop.
Your life was younger than a new piece of clock.
No wonder it didn't fit in my cigarette case.
Your life was a frightened child
and I'd taken it to a prostitute. I was meant
to pet it, not sex it. Someone should have told me
it was fresh from the packet. Someone should have said
it needed shelter and milk, not alcohol and space.
I found it quivering on my sofa-bed, swearing
and itching at nothing. I had damaged it.
I had fed lion heart to a lamb. I thought it had
a knife up its sleeve but it was only a tissue.

So here's the box it came in. Here's the oil can
and the blanket. I stuffed it in a bin liner
but it kept laughing through the plastic. I know
it's alive because it kept opening the door of the van.
My upholstery is littered with bite marks, but
when we hugged goodbye, it clung to my neck
like a vicious koala. Give it a good home
with sponge on the ceiling and plenty of drums.
Tell it I'll send Christmas cards. Tell it I tried,
but being a writer is easier than being a person.
I'm just a torso with a pen and your life has done something
weird to *my* life. Come to think of it…

I have a silent cardboard box beneath my bed.
When was the last time
I took myself out to a restaurant?
In all the kerfuffle, I forgot to check.
Speak to me baby, speak to me.

Hard Times

'Smart move,'
cackled the witch
as I stole our first-born child
from his cot and swapped him for a
cabbage.

Weather Vain

The girl with the August bicycle
gives her bell a cloudless tinkle
but she hasn't got the foggiest.

Grudge

We need reserved seating
at this drink-awareness meeting.
The bloke who hit my bumper
is sitting on my jumper.

Sun Settlers

Evenings are luxurious events
for lovers. The bluebeard moon
yearns inside his grey breath
as women stretch on beaches
and I linger by the twin hammocks
of our home, where sly winds
deal in dandelion confetti
and my love plays music
with sweet-threaded antiquity.
Aria, concerto, requiem, chorale.
I shimmer in the doorway
like a half-remembered silhouette
then, already kissing,
step under the lightbulb.

Later you inquire
about the dirt-rings on my neck,
the jacket tied around my sunburnt forehead.
You inquire why my tonsils taste of coal.
'I just feel guilty', I say,
'for being so happy.'

I'll explain, rewind the clouds.

Earlier that day, in the blond mineral morning,
I woke between the wooden sleepers.
The sun was practising her vowel sounds,
yawning wetly. I edged my eyes
over my corpse, expecting squashed tomato breasts
and baby-food legs, but my body
was a picture of health.
This train-track hadn't been cruised in years. I knew that.

It was a habitude of mine, a quirk,
to lie down once a year
upon the slatted rue of the disused railway,
to sleep the night parallel to any grim steamrolled

horizon and prepare myself
for losing you, my fervent veins,
our mysteries clinking like china cups,
the house we built in the state of happiness.
But of course I always woke,
my train of thought rattled safely by,
my bones unbroken
and today was no different.

The moss gently accused my toes
as I stood, testing the ground.
A white steam engine choo-chooed
across the sky, a duck laughed.
I clambered up onto the train platform
to retrieve my sandals.

I was conscious this was a heavenly town,
rows of lamp-posts like stiff giraffes,
the waspish fruit stalls,
raspberries winking in the bushes
like clotted pearls.
I had lived here half my life,
part-timing in the local factory,
knitting handbags
with swan-neck handles…fake, obviously.
It was finger-dancing work
and I was overpaid.

The town folk, though blissful
seemed forever to be waiting
for travelling salesmen to pass through
and steal their brides, or perhaps
an unmarked lorry of wildebeest
to park up on the village green.

I tied my jacket around my brow
to protect me from the heat and hopped
among the warm shadows of the high street.
Several aborigines were building a rocking chair
from bamboo sticks. The elder, a charcoal-skinned man

with colossal hooped earrings was tweaking the leg
of a ninety-year-old white woman from Swanage.
They were obviously married or at least engaged.

I dodged into a pub called 'Heaven on Earth',
where a wizened soldier was sucking
whisky and lemonade from a conch, I suspected
he was trying to get chucked out,
he kept calling the barmaid 'a spotted toad'
but she just combed her long green hair
and burped, amused.
I acquired myself a stool and sipped a shandy.

A teenage girl dripped through the door
wearing a striped bathing suit
and goggles on her head.
She dried herself with a tea towel
and ordered a steak and kidney pie.
It's an odd sight, such a fit young girl
munching on such stodgy Yorkshire food
but perhaps it had been a very long swim...
six days, she said, but the water
was molten moonlight.

That reminded me to go home.
I left through the stage door.
I don't know why they needed a stage door
in a pub, but apparently people
often gather outside for autographs.
There was a crowd of night-blue anoraks.
They wanted me to sign:
'To Marge, love William', or
'To Darren, love Annie',
their faces looked tired and bereaved
and many were obviously on faulty medication,
some were holding bananas instead of pens
or bits of old twig. I signed for them anyway,
who was I to break the spell?

Evenings are luxurious events
for lovers, the sun rolls
under velvet covers
and the streetlamps revive.
I linger by the twin hammocks
of our home, watch our windows
flutter like angelfish pools.
I see you, head-bopping
to an old cassette. You're
such a slip of a thing,
like pencil-marks, like joy.

The Fall of London

a homage to W.H. Auden's 'The Fall of Rome'

The hottest summer since Eden,
asbos melt on children's legs.
On a laptop fuelled by battery eggs
I type my tiny freedom.

Dumped, he scans the tabloid press
for pictures of his empty bed,
'Our philosophies just clashed,' she said,
while modelling a Gucci dress.

A teacher loads his fountain pen
while schoolgirls snort crystal meth
for parallels of sex and death
in *The Secret Agent*, chapter ten.

The moon cuts herself in half
as Blair, in grave humility
gleaned from the lectern of widescreen TV,
plays with battleships in the bath.

Aspiring saints expel their kids
into a world of stiff unyielding,
Paki-bashing, pitchfork wielding
on streets of weeping caryatids.

Gay priests tossed in the Coliseum
as Jesus Christ our saviour writes
'I just want to meet someone nice',
in spray-paint on his mausoleum.

Fishes oil themselves on beaches,
speckled birds sneeze on the sill,
a doctor takes a sleeping pill
to dream of amulets and leeches.

Altogether elsewhere, I
eat icecream from the tub
in the arms of a new love,
I scoop and sigh.

House and Soul

Been moving house and souls,
this 'For Sale' sign deep in my Rapunzel hair.
Might buy a shoebox, portable,
easy to decorate, could shack up on the seaside
with a plastic windmill flying.

Been deserting twelve and a half friends,
a school like a hairy biscuit
and a dog named Lassie who never came home.
I've already lost touch, it might be under the sofa
or at the back of the big green van. But never mind,
it's not worth much, half a cup
of diluted endearments sucked through a straw.

Been moving house and souls.
Paid a visit to shoebox city
where home is a plastic token for the Big Wheel,
a girl with a firelighter face
and a bloke in a wheelchair claiming
'Strange people *walk* these streets.'

Though shoebox city has its downfalls,
many hungry parents with nothing to gnaw
now their children have scattered.
Things can come slightly unhinged
without doors.

So I'm moving house and souls,
no point crawling, climbing my Rapunzel hair,
you'll only find my head,
but if you care to knock politely on my ribcage,
maybe I'll show you around.

Our Infidelity

Swans were dying in the street, taxis
swerving to avoid their dainty
carcasses and I was sloshing wine
in a badly lit restaurant with a candle,
an ache between my legs and a crack
in the window for the guilt.

This infidelity of ours was so steaming hot
the waitresses were dropping plates, running
their fingers under the cold tap, and swans
– as I said – were exploding by the river.

We didn't need to kiss: the sky had already
started burning, people screaming naked
in gasoline coats through the Christmas lights,
a vicar on a soapbox, somewhere, judging
our souls and a grubby child – an orphan probably –
singing 'Where is love? Is it underneath the willow tree?'

There weren't any willow trees by then,
just smoking stumps and charred mittens
hanging on the air. But you were so beautiful,
it almost didn't matter that a car crashed
every time you smiled. I could almost block out
the sound of sirens and apocalyptic distress.

At the bus stop, I told you – telepathically –
it wasn't our fault: the dead swans,
the seething manholes, the heat. Tomorrow
giant watering cans will drip from cranes
into our respective gardens where our respective
partners will be dancing, wet with innocence.

The Doom

I've been breaking clocks in case they use clocks
in their bombs.

I've been carrying a camouflaged tent
and a brightly coloured tent.

I put salt in my coffee to confuse them.

The chair legs on my chairs are partly sawn.

I have a diamond knuckleduster
to alienate saints disguised as beggars.

I have a few coins in my hat
in case I must pretend to be homeless.

My arm is a fake arm,
I keep my real arm behind my back
and shake with my prosthetic.

I never order the same drink twice
and each drink requires a different
foreign accent and style of limp.

My bed is disguised as a wardrobe
and I sleep on the floor in my neighbour's office
with all the books removed from the bookcase.

I never leave my bookmark on the right page.
Be really careful about the books.

My room is littered with abortion papers, baby clothes,
needles and yoga mats.

Never let them know what you were thinking last.

I carry a bucket of water with me at all times.
No one expects to spontaneously combust.

I carry a Bible and a skipping rope
so people won't know I'm doomed,
but I am, you know I am,
you know I know and everyone else knows,
they're just waiting for how it will happen.

I wish I could go and sit on the dock of the bay
and spy a drowning child
and save that drowning child from drowning.

But I can't move in this full-body body armour.

I can't stay still with all this medicine inside me.
I can't fall in love
in case they're waiting for me to fall in love
so they can attack me in my bridal bed:
doom loves the honeymoon period, it's a bloodbath
and the blood is always tastier
when it's pumping for somebody.

They won't catch me with my trousers down,
I won't be leaving any breadcrumbs or tissues
for them to sniff.

I'm qualified to fornicate with strangers in public lavatories.
Don't let them know you exfoliate.
They can draw spider-diagrams of your morals and motives.

Look
I'm stepping into a taxi with someone
I would never step into a taxi with.
What marvellous deception!

I've been sending formal letters
typed on paper from the Queen's Hotel.

I will never return to the blankets and hearths of my youth.
That is the first place they will look. I am careful
to never ever think what I feel…they have machines for that.

I will bury this notebook next to the grave
of a person I don't admire, then bury a blank one
next to your grave. That is, if you've buried yourself
under your own gravestone, which is always a mistake.

They can do god-awful things with dust these days.
Top of the bill at the déjà vu theatre: *Your Life*
with cynical backing singers and ugly ugly actors.

They have written books disguised as fiction.

We shiver in our flesh.
Don't use words like 'flesh'.
It's their favourite word.

Don't use words. Don't use pictures.
Don't use your head or your heart.

Don't excite the doom.

I am writing myself off.
I am writing myself off.
I am writing myself off.

Perspectives

inspired by the Old English poem 'Deor'

Greg experienced exile through the agency,
worked as a carer, cleaning shit off the walls,
had a daughter called Rose, with yellow hair
who would only eat jam.
He sold this powder made from cactuses
that made his tongue click.
He followed through, and so will she.

For Helen losing the bloke was nothing
to losing the car: a tarmac-trembler
with black-gold windows, coke in the ashtray,
but a piece of her nose fell out in the shower.
She followed through, and so will she.

Carla bought 100 cowboy movies and 200 cans of beer.
It was rodeo week in the TV room.
Marigold took liquid E, then fumbled with this lovely girl
who turned into a massive man.
They followed through, and so will she.

At the university, chaps speak
in words that make people say 'Huh?'
They drink port from little wine glasses.
He can't go back to the grime with the runaways
so he'll follow through, and so will she.

Poetry as a Competitive Sport

We brawl in the bookshops over scraps of bursary.
Firemen flip coins for a burnt child: 'Heads I'm hero!'
Gardeners nibble their neighbour's carrots at midnight.
Musicians pour cola down competing cello holes.

We used to believe in the job itself. Mime artists
built invisible campervans from united limbs,
now they wall themselves into singular boxes.
Chuckles the Clown pissed in Koko's confetti bucket.

With my basket full of severed thumbs, I bumbled back
from the strawberry-picking competition. We'd rather
eat naked cheesecake than share the fruit of our labours,
ever since that little birdie told us a story:

There's a place reserved for you in a horn-gabled hall
where dragons flex their book-spines in shadowy alcoves.
'Come with me,' said the birdie, 'to the Land of Prestige
where the sound of your name carries water from the sun.'

But the moat is soupy with bones, immigrants who rode
by tandem bike or passenger car, ignored the signs:
'IF YOU SHARE A SEAT ON THE FUNICULAR RAILWAY,
PRESTIGE WILL BE DENIED.' Samaritans are labelled.

The locals flaunt Olympian hats on the boardwalk,
enamel-white iPods spurting gunfire in their ears.
Property developers receive upgraded wives
as theatre critics bake in moleskin conservatories

and this is the world of giant sunflowers, big cheese,
the world we swapped a kidney for. I clutch my talent
in the holding room, nose-to-neck with previous friends.
Every time the turnstile clicks, we bubble at the mouth.

Wedding Guest

to be read in an indignant voice

I refuse to curtsey with flowers to the shrine
of getting comfortable on the sofa with a sure-thing.
Tonight I shall be sleeping in a roadhouse
with an individually wrapped bar of soap.

I'm a writer! I lick the curb to taste the whispers
of the pigeons. I drink pints of ketchup.
I don't choose partners by their brand of golf shoe.

Dodgy Harry, he's my friend.
He always keeps some mystery pills in his sock.
'I think this one's a mood stabiliser,' he says,
'How you do feel?'
'I feel alright.'

You can get married if you like. I don't care.
I don't have time for gentle bliss.
I don't have time to poke holes in a potato.

From the Sewer to the Sea: 'A Healing Progress'

a personal melodrama set on the coast

The travel agents warned me this
was not a holiday.
I struck out early May
upon an ancient trail of piss.

My trainers stunk to paradise
through cities void of stars
they call the devil's spas,
where doctors will not treat you twice.

I didn't reach a sickly well
shaped like a stethoscope
with phantom pleas for soap,
instead, like hope, a stronger smell

led me to a chip shop. I thought
the Lord can't have sent me
to kick fish heads gently
in this tacky seaside resort?

The chip-boy wore a gutted face
sanctified in grease,
he offered up a piece
of battered plaice with kingly grace

and suggested a cheap hotel.
I noticed his left hand
defied his command
as it stuttered through his hair gel.

The waterfront was laced with spit
under semi-detached skies,
where neighbourly magpies
varnished their panelled clouds with grit.

The hotel wasn't called 'Spring Falls'
or 'Rest for Weary Ships',
the doors had sliding lips
and the sign spelt 'Crinoline Halls'.

The mini-bar was padlocked tight.
A note on the kettle
read 'No Heavy Metal'.
I unpacked then swallowed the night.

★

When I woke, a militant maid
with bristling arm-hairs
was scrubbing the armchairs,
rows of buckets were on parade.

I ventured out to sniff the air:
saw a child on a bench
beating coins with a wrench,
forging tokens for the funfair.

She opened her cigarette case,
'Here, how about some cigs?'
but it was full of twigs.
'You look needy...what's your disgrace?'

She said, 'Want some coke? skunk? a pill?
...I've got it all right here.'
It was curious gear.
Just a cat on a windowsill.

Looking for cops, she pulled a knife
and grabbed the poor cat's tail.
'I'll fix her with a nail,
then chop off an inch of her life.'

'No,' I said, 'you misunderstand,
I don't get high like that.'
'This is a magic cat!'
she screamed, as I cut loose and ran

to the pier where the fishermen
were strapping crates of gin
to a red rubber ring,
singing, 'Throw her in! Throw her in!'

and the foul ocean was drinking
as trees like old cigars
policed the vacant bars,
slapped the wind for wayward thinking...

    A lone seal is clapping for me.
    His whiskers need a tweeze.
    Where the hell am I please?
    Oh dear, you're in recovery.

            ★

I heal in secret like a cut
on an ant, or a bee.
The graveyard is empty
save for a chaffinch, a stray mutt.

    On a Sunday, marrow farmers
    sip vials of ginger beer
    as market-traders smear
    ointment on their bruised bananas.

The glory-holes are filled with brick,
the jeweller will not sell
hoop earrings to the Belle:
her lobes are nibbled to the quick.

    A masochist sews up the gash,
    douses his burning coals.
    Ex-strippers sell their poles
    back to the blacksmith for hard cash.

Binoculars in the beachhuts
scour the blue and green stain
as new arrivals claim
they survived on piss and peanuts

to reach these golden shores, and pray
they never have to leave.
The seagulls come to grieve
their footsteps if they run away.

Detox

My sleepless one, I'm sending you green tea
across the timelines. Drink for a well-being effect.
I chiselled a bar of soap into a figurine. A figurina.
How's life between backwards forwards hands?
How's life in dirty water my sweet figurina?
I scraped the last grain of soil from my mouth,
been crashing a dodgem around the M1,
the newspapers are made of butter, folk
buttering their toast with stories of suicide
bombers dying from paper-cuts. Death by eye contact.
We're not allowed to look at each other now,
the army supplied us with goggles.
The air is too cold to breathe,
a man with an aerosol comes round once a week.
The bananas are straight like beanpoles
from the stress. The maps are wrong.
They found the leg of a car mechanic under a car.
The streets tinkle with light jazz rain,
the bus shelters flicker like holograms,
one in ten people are invisible,
I walked through a woman on London Bridge,
I wouldn't have known but my clothes were silted
with spit and I felt like I'd just been ice skating.
My best friend got pregnant six times
in the last month, and already her kids have left school
and built their own car parks in the heart of New York.
The life expectancy of a fly is one second.
The human brain is dirty and infects the blood
with 'gongbellchimus', a contagious disease that causes
the patient to believe they have a large amount of gold
inside their ribcage. Rome could now be built
in a day, using lasers, plasticine. Sometimes
I feel like one tiny lightbulb in a huge flashing poster
advertising peanuts. I've been avoiding food with additives.
Government officials in dentist's chairs wearing face-packs
and reading philosophy. Everyone is toned. Toned hair.
Toned noses. Free mineral juice. They're calling it 'The Grand Detox'.
I found a ring on the road, which I put on my hand.

Poet in the Class

I read the poem about Bobby
who climbed the mountain,
who reached the peak and jumped,
who noticed half-way down
the filing-paper wings were far too weak.
I read the poem of the eighth sea,
the one they never tell you about.
I read the poem of the shout
across the desert
heard only by the sandstorms.
I read the poem of the one-legged horse
who tried to stand up for himself.
I read the poem of the hard-working elf
who poisoned Santa's tea
and said, 'You never make presents for me.'

Afterwards, I apologised. Really I did.
Better vitamin-children
than sherbet-fountain hooligans.
Rhyming-couplet poetry
would keep them in their lines.
Poets are cockroaches, they only sound good
when you crunch them.
The teacher smiled at this, lukewarm handshake.

She had put me in the second-best chair,
the one with the fingernail marks
along the varnish:
We have a poet in the class today,
come to read some modern poetry,
not what we're used to
but I'm sure we'll cope.
Aren't we lucky to be here?
Sit still.

I frowned and put my pride to my lips, inhaled
some pencil-sharpenings,
sneezed, then began.

Blame the Poodle

Like the girl who dropped her ice cream
down a volcano and leaped in after it,
too warm for comfort, I realised mid-air

that my chances were gone, the second
I entangled in the lead of a passing poodle
and swore myself purple. I was recording

a message on your answering machine
at the time. You'll never call me now.
Like the girl who forgot to let go

of her balloon and now orbits the earth,
I realised completely – smack-bang,
blue-in-the-face, cold-water clarity –

the second it was too far to jump.
I blame the poodle for everything.
For the thumping eyes on the long walk

back where every step was a slump,
after swapping symbols – a cheap, metal
turn-your-skin-green necklace

I never took off. Turned left at the station,
a street before the verge of tears.
I blame the poodle for the morning

when a bouncer chucked me out
of my own dream, my hair was a party hat
and the gap in the teeth widened.

I blame the poodle for the images
that are about to get worse. Sometimes they do.
They creep like mannequins,

throb through the memories that put me to bed
on nights when my brain is a runway
lined with twitching red lights, and the thunder

scrapes her blackened violin.
Did you hear the one about the girl
who slept beneath her pillow?

The tooth fairy hacked off her head.

I didn't see that one coming. I'm sorry
Lords and Ladies. I'm sorry
gentle reader. I must learn from my mistakes

like the girl who played with matches,
like the girl who chopped another girl
in half, then forgot the trick.

Poor Little Miss Guided
skipping across minefields with a basket.
Put war in a pretty dress and call it peace.

You're breaking and entering my poem, dammit!
Throats full of poodles and steadfast
forgetfulness. We're always indulging time.

I blame the poodle for the puddle
I poured over the coat you lay down for me.
I blame the poodle for the chronic sunrise

that squints in my eyes as I bow,
collect flowers, shake hands,
unroll the red guilt and swagger down.

Short Story

If I was a person, like my granddad, who picked one partner
and boiled them tea for the rest of my days, smiling supportively,
I wouldn't have cheated. At least, I wouldn't have cheated
with such a downright skank.

I bet my granddad never came home and threw a fit
at my grandma because she asked him 'Where've you been?'
Cheaters don't like being asked where they've been.
That makes them angry.

Cheaters don't like it when you sniff their clothes,
or check their phones, or cook a lovely dinner, saying,
'Is it something I've done?' That makes cheaters feel
rotten inside, like an egg full of blood.

This morning, you rustled up an English breakfast
while I had a long, long shower. 'The bacon's soggy,'
I said before I'd even tasted it, steering my walking
cliché to the car. I didn't cry until I reached the lights.

Lunacy

I got to the cloud. I picked the highest
banana. I peeled it right in your face
and I said, 'Ha!'

But then you got to the moon, muscled
your gorgeous sculpted belly up the pole
and started flicking peanuts.

Now I'm just coughing cloud-mist
with my limp banana.

And every Tom, Dick and Harry's got a cloud.
It's like the Victorian slums. I've got hoof-marks
on my lip from sleeping top-to-tail
with a pit pony.

When I was a nipper, my daddy
told me bullies never reach the moon.
He said they'd be crying into their microwave dinners,
watching me peel my triumphant banana
from the highest cloud.

Now the moon's full of bullies.
They've built their own colony. They grow
diamond-shaped lettuces, raise children
with skin as smooth as Sellotape,
and down here, on cloud-terrace, we get
their daily broadcast on the tannoy:
'HA!' it says, and 'HA!'

All the ones who gave you Chinese burns,
skinned your teddies, made you writhe in angry
lust. They're all there, spitting tenners,
having a ball.

And we've just got to be happy.
Not for them, obviously, but for ourselves.

The Perfect Man

Narcissus went to the pool.
Mothers were tossing boomerangs in the park,
fathers were catching them in their teeth.
Narcissus sat on the bank and hugged his knees, remembered
the kids he went to school with –
some had set up novelty jewellery shops
in the hollows of the Mediterranean,
some had turned into almond trees
or perished, snake-bitten and hoarse, whispering love songs.
He knew about the sleep of death,
when sweet music spoils inside your ear
and one night you call your dealer on the telephone,
ask for a storm to scatter your fleet.
Narcissus ran his fingers down his face, retraced
his ex-lovers:
beautiful birds with the heads of women
who stuffed their tail feathers in his plughole, shrieking:
'You never listen, Narcissus, it's always about you!'
And the boys – dim, blank-looking boys
who marvelled their tongues along his jaw-line,
then went back to class.
His ex-lovers were really not lovers at all.
Except one.

She arrived at the worst time,
he'd rented a hotel room,
started drinking the mini-bottles of conditioner,
anything to smooth his soul.
She had pinballed from commune to commune,
humiliating herself in karaoke bars
singing 'Mr Bojangles',
and was looking for somewhere to bury her head.
Narcissus loved her, front-way and back-way,
with all the speed in his spluttering engine.
They staggered around, laughing, pretending
to be free. But this wasn't Paris. Paris isn't Paris.
When they tangled, he could hear his heart
bleeding inside her.

He changed her name. He called her Echo.
It was funny at first.
'Echo! Make my dinner!'
'Narcissus! Make my dinner!'
But one minute they were touching hands
across the massive tablecloth, then
the candles torched the duvet, the bread rolls
jammed the toilet pipes, the forks
split their lips and the knives severed the rest.
And all he could say was 'You did this!'
And all she could say was 'You did this!'
They packed their bags simultaneously.
The last thing he needed
was someone exactly like him.

He got a job in a factory,
checking cabbages for worms,
checking his hands for liver spots.
He flew home to watch his mother die,
attached to a drip
in a very westernised hospital,
you could buy microwave hamburgers
from the vending machine…
a far cry from her sea-nymph days,
when she would drag men upstairs by the length of their ties
and Narcissus, a little boy, would hear
the roar of the ocean through the wall.

Now here he was, on this grassy verge,
by the oak tree
which once sported his tyre-swing.
Narcissus, a grown man,
with stretchmarks on his heart,
looking down into the pool
at his own face.
His eyes, clear blue and radiantly sad.
His skin, untouched by the wind
that rattled through his bones.
Narcissus splashed his lips against the water
and tried, he really tried,
to love himself.

Reminder Notice

Friday, she's as good as new.
The weekend strips the trees.
Monday, tight as a screw.

Daily bread is buttered blue
by clipboard companies.
Friday, she's as good as new.

In the lift, a smile or two
grazes her employees.
Monday, tight as a screw.

Heat blisters-up the glue
on cheaply framed CVs.
Friday, she's as good as new.

Moonlight doesn't misconstrue
drunks with good degrees.
Monday, tight as a screw.

Post your soggy poems through
the railings of the breeze.
Friday, she's as good as new.
Monday, tight as a screw.

Mr Bird

My daddy eats egg whites and tuna, his muscles
are bigger than my mother, his new tattoo
has its own weightlifting programme, his bald head
is bowling down the skittles of his sighs,
he might buy a sports car and that's fine.

He cushioned the climbing frame
with his sponge philosophy, as a kid
I bounced the frontiers on a summer spotless knee.
The other dads had Dobermanns, kept their kids
in man-sized mousetraps, self-destructing
toothpaste caps, doors cracked open with the nozzle
of a baking tray, metal files in birthday cakes, slept
with one foot on the phone, the mummies carried flick knives
to the neighbourhood watch meetings, but *we* didn't need a nanny
in a bulletproof pinny, cricket bats or bolted catflaps,
we had daddy. The balloon behind my army mother,
silent pen on schooling slips. When the hood of my jacket
was weighed down with stones, he slipped that puny potion
in my pride, the potion that took twenty years
to fit inside my blood.

And now he's pumping iron in the mid-life
of his protein shake, defeating all the kids
who never picked him for the football team
and we both know how bizarre we are, skinny spooks in helmets.
My mother is a monkey doctor, breaking comas with bananas,
my brother is a ballet dancer, spinning gold from straw pyjamas.
I'm a jumped-up pony with an eye for the abyss,
but my daddy is a bodybuilder and he built this
and I'm very pleased to welcome Mr Bird.

Flat Mate

My shadow rolled up her loose, grimy sleeves,
slid off the stool where I was sipping juice,
picked my pocket with a hooked finger,
crept back with bagels and a worse habit.

My shadow stayed faithful until lunchtime,
watched GMTV upside down in bed,
clicked the wheel of her lighter and vanished.
The air span with stringy, puckered habits.

I'm not her mother. I can't stalk her
from streetlight to dustbin in muted shoes.
She ducked back through the catflap for dinner,
chewing on black winegums and her meek leer.

My shadow pressed a hot-water bottle
against my ruptured side and tucked me in.
Her mobile phone shivered like a habit.
A shred of stocking caught in the flung door.

My shadow dragged another shadow home,
their eyes dilated with rotten sunlight.
I slept under the bed with the secrets,
watching bedsprings flinch from their ghostly weight.

In the morning, I packed my clean notebooks.
my crisp underwear, my health magazines.
My shadow called me a fair-weather friend.
She scoffed: 'You want to live like a palm tree?

You want to walk with redheads on the beach,
drink milk with men in white suits, and smugly
pride yourself on being ashamed of me?'
I fumbled the doorknob with my limp wrist.

Shadowless, the following years were a blur.
Blessings dissolved on my tongue like habits.
A degree, a smoke-free house, two bright kids,
a sundial in the backyard, chiming noon.

Hours before my death, I found my shadow
frozen stiff on the swing-seat, skeletal.
Her feet were webbed from walking. Rejection
had fattened her habits, suckled her bones.

I offered up. Let her prepare my lids
with warpaint, shade my ribs with murmurs,
clip my door keys to her belt. When night came
I lay beneath our cradle, cowering.

The University Poetry Society

a tract hopefully designed to offend almost all aspiring laureates

Come to the university poetry society. Pull up a poof.
A girl with Catholic guilt will take your name.
Post-drinks, there'll be 'readings from the floor',
(don't say 'open mic', we're not in Camden,
and don't jump around like those performance plebs
who speak from the 'gut' in their urban dives.
Use an Elizabethan voice. Lift your nose
like a prince about to spurt phlegm. That's right.)
This month's theme is 'creation', so the Book
of Genesis is an obvious inspiration, or the ancient
Greek muses. Serious verse is appreciated
(last week a boy read a poem about Slush Puppies.
Miranda called security).

I know your type: calling 'rap music' poetry,
praising honesty above excellence, squiggling
song lyrics with skateboarders outside prisons,
making it 'fun'. That won't impress us here
at the university poetry society. I'm published too:
The Palindrome of Paradise, an educated, yet
oddly titillating, work about a dyslexic monk,
written entirely backwards. After your reading,
I'll run my regular session, 'hanging with the greats',
where I pretend to be Lord Byron in this wig.

I've got more flair than most public school boys,
I've leapt train-barriers wearing a kimono, had my
fair share of fanny, mixed a White Russian, so you
can't shock me with your caustic tales of sexual
deviance. I've peeped inside a Job Centre, I'm hip
to the working class. I would simply dispute
the fascination of such things. Personally, I think
poetry should elevate us above the mundane: good god,
if shop assistants start reading poetry for pleasure then
surely we, as an institution, have failed to maintain

the vigorous intellectualism of our art. If we listened
to you, we'd be overrun by dinner ladies and hod-carriers
asking us to explain complicated metaphors, drawing
moustaches on the portraits of our most eminent scholars,
soiling our antique chairs with their enormous, pocketed
coats. NO, I say. I WILL NOT ENDURE IT!

I'd like to end the evening with a poem I wrote for
my sister. As a toddler I pet-named her 'Anne of Cleves'
after Henry the Eighth's unsightly fourth wife, I regret
it now, but kids will be kids:

Inverted Dreams
by Clarence Sharpenwell

> *Thoughts, citrus, antiseptic bony thoughts*
> *are cracking, like ice, on the windowsill*
> *of my melancholic mournings,*
> *the tulips are crying, sister, rusticated*
> *from their spring term, oh why, oh why,*
> *do you persist on meeting that woman?*
> *Are you a lesbian, sister?*
> *Do not fiddle the illicit harp of destiny*
> *for her music will be twangy.*
> *Also, mother will have a nervous breakdown.*

Thank you so much for coming. Miranda
has provided nibbles in the foyer. I think
we even have Bombay Mix. Risqué.

I Married Green-Eyes

I married Green-Eyes early last July.
The neighbours all advised me to go green.
Grass smells sweeter when the gooseberries cry.
The butcher-boy went green when he got clean.

Debra married Blue-Eyes straight after school.
The neighbours all advised me to go green.
Blue-Eyes rubs his trunks in the local pool.
The au pair tops his blueberries with cream.

Stuart found his Brown-Eyes in a sports car.
He'd seen suspicious bruises on her thigh.
There she was, with Silver-Tongue and Knife-Scar.
Grass smells sweeter when the gooseberries cry.

'Keep away from White-Eyes and the drug scene,'
her wild-eyed mother begged her, 'Please don't wed:
the butcher-boy went *green* when he got clean.'
White-Eyes and White-Eyes honeymooned in bed.

Streamers webbed the streets like celery string.
With colours of the world, they dyed the sky.
Our neighbours believed each confetti-fling
that fell to pieces, early last July.

Familiar Ground

Red Riding Hood went back to the spot
where she was nearly mauled,
and she waited.

A hairy man in a hat
asked her for a cigarette.

She tilted down her sunglasses,
gave him a peek
of her bloody black eyes.

'Jesus Christ,' he said,
'what happened to you?'

'Rottweilers, bears, gorillas,' she said,
'lions, tigers…pigeons even,
they've all taken a shot.
By the way, sonny, I know who *you* are.'

'You've changed,' he said, 'you're sharper,
wiser, I can see that.'

Then he offered her a bottle
and she drank like an outlaw
until her eyes rolled back in her head.

The wolf dragged her body to a clearing
and they were not separated.

When dawn broke, she regained consciousness.

The wolf was leaning by an oak, looking sweaty.
It had been too easy.

Red Riding Hood smiled a cough
and wiped her mouth.
'I must have nodded off,' she said,
'I didn't do anything daft last night did I?'

'No,' said the wolf, 'you were charming.'

'Oh good,' she said
and staggered off through the trees,
her dress tucked into her tights.

Women in Progress

an exultation for the fourteen-year-old girls in my poetry workshops

Gemma would take her hair-straighteners
to a desert island but she's no stereotype.
I hope she nails her sonnet and that lad in 2009.

Maxie has a puppy dog hidden
in the kennel of her chest. Publicly
she thumps her jewellery, roaring, 'Your mum!'
I hope she acts herself in 2009.

Salena's best friend betrayed her. Now
she must audition new friends in the lunch hall.
I hope she finds hundreds in 2009.

Zoe shields her largeness with her library books
– Point Horror – walks the weaker kids home
through the path of least bullies.
I hope her mum gets better in 2009.

People think Rachel's got a Loser badge
pinned to her hoodie but I've read her poetry
and she's got the perfect simile for sky.
I hope she goes to sixth form in 2009.

Because you'll break my heart, 2009,
if you show me again those tired teachers flexing red pens.
And a drowning poet saying, 'You could be anything'
to an oversized class in an undersized room.
Don't show me the future in their faces:
girls waving pom-poms at the fringes of the football field,
girls feeling fat behind tills. A knockers joke
in every Christmas cracker. Tell an honest one, 2009.
Tell me the one about the woman
who dug a tunnel through the system and set forth.
She had panda-eyes but an independent tear.

Sky News

*Looking back from this distance of time and without reliable
documentary evidence, it is hard to know if what follows is
legend or fact. Suffice it to say that the story of the extraordi-
nary and massive 'firework', as these explosive objects were
known, is well attested down the centuries, references to it
coming from numerous sources. The giant 'firework' may or
may not have been responsible for the destruction of the
'Moon', which was the name given to the secondary and
much smaller natural satellite which orbited Planet Earth for
four and a half billion years, but it is as good an explanation
as any for its disappearance. For further information on the
'Legend of the Giant Firework' consult the relevant entry in
the Encyclopaedia Galactica.*

The dusk was crisp as a fifty-pound note,
automatic doors of toyshops opening and closing
like dumb-struck mouths, crisp packets roaming
the streets with salt on their breath. A snowman
melted to the ground, took a big breath, then
stood up again. Tonight was the night.

The firework Greenpeace tried to ban.
The firework pickled in the pharaoh's fist, stuffed
in the highest cupboard of Einstein's dreams, sketched
in secret leaflets tucked into the windscreen wipers
of 747s by political activists. The firework that defies
science: underwater fire-extinguishers slipped into
the pockets of the coral reef. The firework tattooed
on Nostradamus' ankle, spied in the swirls
of Michelangelo's muesli, cut from
the Old Testament for being too fanciful.
The big boy, the real deal, the final countdown.

At eight o'clock precisely mankind ran out
like a rich kid on Christmas day with a new
life-size Wendy house, climbed astride hill

and phone box, proud as flags, trained
their gaze on the up, up, up.

A fleck of light flicked into the eve
followed by a shining blue line –
the stripe in the toothpaste – bleaching
a trail through the black.

The moon was asleep without a care in the world,
the doorknob to the sky, minding her own.
Down here, on earth, governments started biting their nails,
pointing their useless remote controls at the heavens.
But it was too late.
The angels stopped kissing, wiped their mouths in disgust,
God hid under the table with his fingers in his ears.
From Hawaii to Hartlepool, the cry went up
as the moon fell down.

There was a small pop, like a birthday surprise,
darkness leapt from a cake and swallowed the room,
aeroplanes tumbled from fiery bedclothes. It started to hail.
Big hunks of moonstone, the size of children's
ABC blocks, but harder and aflame.
People aimed their hosepipes at the sky,
ran around, lost in their own backyards.

NASA tried to build a new one from headlamps
and foil, but it was neon like a vending machine.
A bloke with some bruises claimed to be
'the man on the moon', tried to get compensation
for his fall. A moonstone vase was stolen
from the British Museum, nicked back, then stolen
again. Astrologers went on strike
to the consternation of few. Stephen Hawking said
we'd be kicked from the sun, freeze in a snowball
but the earth stood its ground, fixed like a prejudice.

Like blowing an eyelash from the palm of your hand
to make a wish
we must release things into the air.

The consequences, my dear, belong to history.
So you mustn't blame the people, or the firework,
for the death of the moon.

Now, she is almost a myth
like the dragon, a joke like the chocolate kettle.
Lovers are fine with their dull candlelit dinners:
a little less romance, a little less sparkle,
the tideless sea like an angry puddle. Tom Cruise
is hot as hell in his latest film *Galaxy Busters*.
The Queen bought her own private cloud
to hover by the gates like a chauffeur. A motorway
replaced the Milky Way. 'Kellogg's Cornflakes' written
in mist across the daybreak. Sticks of dynamite
advertised in *Vogue* as stylish housewarming gifts,
and there are rumours of a secret mission,
Operation SUNDOWN or the allusive RED ROCKET.
Anyhow, firework factories have been working
at a race-winning pace. They say, Bonfire Night this year
will be a real show-stopper.

With thanks to St Hild's School, Hartlepool.

Closet Affair

When the shivers of shame have stopped, she said,
I'll just hop on a bus and go back to my husband
but first – this might sound odd – I want to sit
in your airing cupboard for a couple of hours.
The mortgage payments will be modest
and you have to knock if you want to come in
and I'll say, 'Who is it?'
and you'll say, 'I've brought you a cup of tea'
and I'll say, 'Leave it on the doorstep please, I'm in the shower.'
But, of course, I won't be.
I'll just be sitting there in the dark.

Inner-city Plot

The earth won't spare a seed.
Tomatoes die on the allotments.
A midwife flips a wild card.
The placenta tastes like talent.
She swipes the barcode of the future
with a baby the size of a beer can.

Parents, solid as a beer can,
high on sunflower seeds,
unveil their deckchairs to the future
as woodlice fry on the allotments
and the toddler walks! Such talent!
Our stumbling, pink-nosed wild card.

In skateboarding parks, wild cards
spin on their heads like beer cans,
hard children smash their talent
though windscreens, spitting glass seeds,
as bag ladies drift the allotments
singing 'Don't feed the future'.

Pale teachers paste the future
between laminated wild cards,
but she takes her class on the allotments
digging for Viking beer cans,
coins and golden pomegranate seeds
to swap for a beanstalk of talent.

Youth workers scout for talent
by the pool tables, green as future,
rolling with red and yellow seeds,
and their pamphlets, sly as wild cards,
whisper 'Problem with the beer can?'
but youth clubs hustle the allotments.

Sniffer dogs raid the allotments
for wraps of buried talent,
as shooting stars splutter like beer cans:
bu…bu…be careful in the future,
but cashpoints gobble wild cards
and the earth won't spare a seed.

The future sows your wild card seeds
all over the allotments, rain falls
like talent, beer cans rise.

The Alcoholic Marching Song

His first pint lasted for years, a lullaby
from a stranger who never disapproved
of luscious birds and hop-head bees
sipping from his head, the tang of brains.

When parents descended on strings
like puppets from the past, he could
always dispel them, drink his own
advice, went down lovely, hiccup.

A million miles from the old girl
in the ladies' bog who couldn't borrow
an eye liner pencil because no one
wanted their lead on her greasy ducts.

After all, when he relapsed,
the binmen still came on a Wednesday,
he didn't raise his glass
and find it sparkling with blood.

For every nip of vodka, he nipped
a problem in the bud. Piss easy.
Bobbly friends with static jumpers
warming their whisky cockles.

A million miles from the old boy
on the morning train who drew
a face on his knee with a fag butt
and told it to cheer up, ashy bastard.

What did they expect anyway?
Him to sit in stale coffee rooms
with a bunch of dry crones, dredging
up old porkies, old faux pas?

He's sailing. He's taming the floor
in a spinning bed. He won't fly
the white flag until he's done
a million, a million miles at least.

Company of Women

I come from a company of women
who put their elbows on the table, worship the wine,
adjust their Versace sundials
to Greenwich Mean Time: 'I've just come back
from a very interesting period of my life.'
Their husbands are chanting commentators,
wear soft shirts, stub their toes easily.
Women live in the shadow of women,
orate the broadsheets over breakfast:
'I hear they're making a musical
of *Tristan and Isolde*. Can you imagine?'
But sometimes their eyes meet
through a fish tank, during a record
of 'God Bless the Child'.
They've all been slammed against a wall
at some point, loved a drunk, found their breasts
several miles from home.
And backstage, when the restaurants are empty,
I gather my leads, devise
a family.

XI Tyrant

When I was born, the tyrant wrapped a red ribbon
round my throat and whispered, 'If you remove this
your head will fall off.'

When I was nine, I removed the ribbon and my
head stayed put, but people's grandparents began to die.

My first engagement ring, when I was fifteen,
looked like a clipping of pipe. The tyrant said,
'If you remove this, your hands will wither.'

When I was seventeen, I flicked the ring
down the drain and my hands were lithe as minnows
but fat girls were shaking like wet tractors everywhere.

When I met X, a nut loosened in the tyrant's neck,
'If you apply this, love will Tippex your career.'
X made me happy and the tyrant didn't like it.

I caught the tyrant eating my UCAS forms.
'I only want what's best for you,' the tyrant said
through a mouthful of pulped ambition.

At twenty, my tyrant begot ten baby tyrants
sworn to the Bad News Bible. X was badly wounded.
'If you salvage this, we'll leave you
for dead,' the tyrants said.

But tough as roman numerals, X and I
stormed the aisle. Just truth, no brutal prayers.

When we grew up, the tyrants looped a rainbow
through a black hole and said,
'If you remove this, you will topple.'

We removed the rainbow, when we were serene,
and without rings, ribbons or rainbows, we clung on.

A Love Song

Long before we tie the knot, Divorce moves in.
He sits on the naughty step, patting his knees.

Crowned in towel, I step out the shower
and he's there, handing me a raffle ticket.

He plays kickabout with the neighbourhood kids,
chalks crosses on their doors and buys them Big Macs.

Socking his fist into the bowl of his hat,
he'd kicked the gate wide, that sunny day in Leeds.

My mum was incredulous, 'She's only ten,
she can't possibly have made contact with you.'

He clocked my young face and handed me his card.
'Call me when you fall in love, I'm here to help.'

Perhaps he smelt something in my pheromones,
a cynicism rising from my milk teeth.

With gum, he stuck notes on Valentine's flowers:
tiny life-letters in factual grey ink.

The future cut two keys for a new couple.
On my twenty-first, Divorce took the spare room.

He loves to breathe down the spout of the kettle,
make our morning coffee taste mature and sad.

He waits by the car, slowing tapping Tic-Tacs
down his throat. We've thought about stabbing him,

but he's such a talented calligrapher:
our wedding invitations look posh as pearl.

He bought us this novelty fridge magnet set,
a naked doll with stick-on wedding dresses.

Divorce and I sometimes sit in the kitchen,
chucking odd magnetic outfits at the fridge.

He does the cooking, guarding over the soup,
dipping his ladle like a spectral butler.

He picks me daisies, makes me mix-tapes, whispers,
'Call me D,' next thing he'll be lifting the veil.

After the honeymoon, we'll do up the loft,
give Divorce his own studio apartment.

We must keep him sweet, my fiancée agrees,
look him in the eye, subtly hide matches,

remember we've an arsonist in the house.
The neighbours think we're crazy, pampering him

like a treasured child, warming his freezing feet,
but we sing Divorce to sleep with long love songs.